BATMAN BEYOND

THE ANIMATED SERIES GUIDE

LONDON, NEW YORK, MELBOURNE,
MUNICH, AND DELHI

Series Editor Alastair Dougall
Series Designer Robert Perry
Art Director Mark Richards
Publishing Manager Cynthia O'Neill Collins
Category Publisher Alex Kirkham
Production Nicola Torode
Dtp Designer Dean Scholey

This title was designed and edited by Tall Tree Limited

First American Edition, 2004
03 04 05 06 07 10 9 8 7 6 5 4 3 2 1

Published in the United States by DK Publishing, Inc.
375 Hudson Street, New York, New York 10014

DK Publishing, Inc. offers special discounts for bulk purchases for sales promotions or premiums. Specific, large-quantity
needs can be met with special editions, including personalized covers, excerpts of existing guides, and corporate imprints.
For more information, contact Special Markets Department, DK Publishing, Inc., 375 Hudson Street, New York, NY 10014
Fax: 800-600-9098.

Library of Congress Cataloging-in-Publication Data

Beatty, Scott, 1969-.
  Batman Beyond : the animated series guide / written by Scott Beatty.--
1st American ed.
     p. cm. -- (Animated series guides)
  Includes index.
  ISBN 0-7566-0586-5 (PLC)
  1. Batman beyond (Television program)--Juvenile literature. I. Title.
II. Series.
  PN1992.77.B352B43 2004
  791.45'72--dc22

                              2004005005

Reproduced by Media Development and Printing, UK
Printed and bound in Italy by L.E.G.O.

Visit DC Comics online at www.dccomics.com or at keyword DC Comics on America Online.

see our complete product line at
www.dk.com

BATMAN
BEYOND
THE ANIMATED SERIES GUIDE

DK

CONTENTS

GREETINGS FROM NEW GOTHAM

Gotham City has changed, and not necessarily for the better. This teeming metropolis has always been mired in crime and corruption. But in the past, Gotham could count on its Dark Knight defender to put evil in its place. Then, one day in the not-so-distant future, Batman simply disappeared. Without a word to Gotham's citizens, Bruce Wayne hung up the Caped Crusader's cowl and Utility Belt for good. The Batmobile gathered dust in the Batcave. And whatever hope was left in Gotham was soon replaced by despair.

That was then. Now, a new Batman has emerged to bring law to the lawless. Gotham is bigger and badder. Its buildings are taller, towering nearly a mile above the mean streets of the old city. Flying cars careen through concrete canyons with neon vid-screens flashing in the dark. Street gangs terrorize. Corporate tyrants oppress. The Dark Knight couldn't have come back at a better time.

But he isn't Bruce Wayne. No, this Batman is Terry McGinnis, a teenaged Tomorrow Knight determined to launch a new offensive in the war on crime. Bruce provides back-up, while this young avenger is fitted out with an awesome new arsenal to battle evil. And although the Rogues Gallery has changed, Batman's mission remains the same: to protect the innocent from fiendish foes!

END OF THE BAT?

Batman spent decades fighting an endless war on crime. As time wore on, an aging Bruce Wayne relied more and more on technology to win fights as the Dark Knight. Then, one night, he picked up a gun to stop a crazed criminal. What had Batman become?

Ion particles glow blue as Batman's gauntlet energizes for a strike!

FIST OF FURY

Batman began to slow down as he got older. To keep up with the younger criminals, the Dark Knight built new weapons to give him an added advantage over his adversaries.

NEW BATSUIT

The Dark Knight eventually built an entire super-charged Batsuit. His new armor was darker and more frightening than the old costume.

In his search for kidnapped debutante Bunny Vreeland, the suit increased his strength and agility to new levels.

WHACK-! KRAS

BATMAN'S SUPER-CHARGED gauntlet and experimental exo-skeleton helped him pack an even bigger punch than before. Terrified thugs now faced a real Super-Bat !

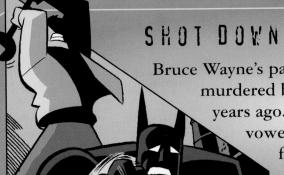

SHOT DOWN

Bruce Wayne's parents were murdered by a gunman many years ago. As Batman, Bruce vowed never ever to use a firearm, even to save his own life. Unfortunately, it was a promise he was destined to break.

BRUCE WAS SO ASHAMED of himself for brandishing a gun that he sealed up Batman's costume in a display case. The Dark Knight was officially retired. "Never again," he vowed. "Never again."

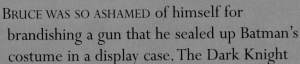

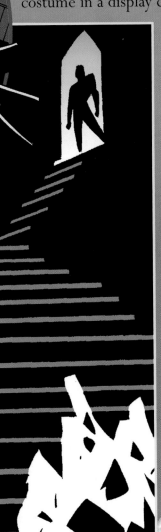

SHUT-IN

Bruce left the Batcave and retreated to his home in Wayne Manor above. There he lived alone with his loyal dog, Ace. His friend and valet Alfred Pennyworth had died many years before. From now on, Gotham City would be without its guardian Dark Knight.

BAT DATA

• Bruce was only ~~ten~~ years old when his parents were killed by a mugger.

• When he retired, Batman no longer had any loyal partners to help him fight crime.

A New Dark Knight

Twenty years after Bruce's retirement, events would unfold to create a new Batman. Terry McGinnis was in the right place at the right time to defend Bruce from a gang of Jokerz. The incident made a lasting impression on both. Like Bruce Wayne, Terry McGinnis would tragically lose his father. And, like Bruce, Terry would seek justice as Batman!

TERRY McGINNIS

Before his father died, Terry McGinnis only cared about having fun. Although he was basically a good kid, Terry's quick temper often got him into fights. Sadly, he argued with his dad on the last night Warren McGinnis was alive.

WARREN McGINNIS worked in the research division of the Wayne-Powers Corporation. When Warren's friend Harry uncovered the illegal production of nerve gas at the company, he gave Warren a computer disk detailing every sinister secret.

PAYBACK

Terry blamed himself for leaving his father at home defenseless. But he didn't have much time to mourn. Terry discovered the computer disk and the secrets Warren McGinnis died to protect.

TERRY KNEW that wealthy Derek Powers could bribe the authorities to prevent an inquiry. The young man needed an ally, someone above the law. But would Bruce Wayne be willing to help Terry bring Powers to justice?

A NEW BEGINNING...

Bruce listened patiently to Terry's story. He advised Terry to take the disk to Commissioner Barbara Gordon and let the police handle Powers. However, Terry had a different kind of solution in mind...

CONTRARY TO Bruce's wishes, Terry took the Batsuit and went after Derek Powers himself. After two decades, Batman struck again! The Tomorrow Knight swooped into a Wayne-Powers warehouse and shut down its dangerous nerve gas production line!

SMACK!

Oof!

JOB OPPORTUNITY

Bruce Wayne was impressed by Terry's skills in the Batsuit. Terry's mother thought Wayne was offering her son a job. If she only knew the truth about his new after-school career...

BAT DATA

• Powers's henchman **Mr. Fixx** murdered Terry's father.

• **Mr. Fixx** died battling the new Batman.

WITH BRUCE'S APPROVAL, Terry became the new Batman. Soon, the Batcave would be fully operational again. And a new war on crime would begin!

THE NEW BATSUIT

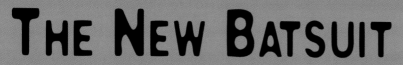

Bruce Wayne built the new Batsuit nearly 20 years ago. It was high-tech then and remains cutting edge in the year 2038. Just look at all the weapons packed inside this sleek costume!

The Batsuit is linked to Terry's nervous system and increases his strength by ten.

BATWINGS

The Batsuit's retractable wings enable Batman to glide silently and unnoticed through Gotham City at night, just like a bat.

Synaptic controls allow Batman to operate many of the Batsuit's functions by thought alone!

CAN YOU BELIEVE that Batman hears with his fingers? Audio receivers in the gloves of the Batsuit allow the Tomorrow Knight to pick up distant sounds or eavesdrop on faraway conversations.

Wings fold up inside the costume when not in use.

THIEF TRAP

Bruce Wayne cleverly booby-trapped the Batsuit so that no one could steal it. If the wrong person dons the costume, Bruce can paralyze the wearer instantly by remote control!

BAT DATA

• Audio implants in the cowl keep Batman in constant radio contact with Bruce Wayne.

• The Batsuit is bulletproof and resistant to heat and cold, but not radiation.

INVISIBLE TOUCH

By pressing a button on the buckle of his control belt, Batman can become virtually invisible. The Batsuit will blend into any background and is perfectly camouflaged.

BAT-VISION

Infrared optical sensors in Batman's cowl help him to view distant objects clearly in the dark. Video links to the Batcave allow Bruce Wayne to see whatever Terry McGinnis sees, giving the young man an added advantage in fight situations.

This Batman can fly with boot-jets propelling him at high velocites!

ROCKET thrusters built into his boots allow Batman to blast off and out of danger. With his magnetic soles, Batman can cling to metal ceilings or even walk up walls!

TERRY HAS spent many hours examining the circuitry inside the Batsuit. He carries a set of special tools so that he can repair any damage or malfunctions right on the spot.

BAT-GADGETS

In addition to his battling Batsuit, the Tomorrow Knight has a flying Batmobile that he drives both down and *above* the mean streets of Gotham City! He also has a new generation of cool gadgets tucked into his Utility Belt to help him win the war on crime!

ROCKET-WING

A nifty new vehicle in Batman's arsenal, the Rocket-Wing is a jet-propelled skateboard. It is easily maneuverable between the skyscrapers of Gotham's concrete canyons.

BATMAN TRACKS crooks with a rocket-fired homing device launched from his glove. The device is magnetized in order to stick to fleeing getaway cars.

COLLAPSIBLE Batarangs are concealed inside Batman's gauntlets. With a flick of his wrist, Batman can shoot these like lasers and shock his foes silly!

FOR CLOSE-UP video surveillance, Batman sometimes takes a sneak peek with night-vision Bat-Binoculars.

BATMOBILE

The Batmobile has always been Batman's preferred mode of transportation. The Tomorrow Knight's vehicle is a fast-flying car with all sorts of offensive and defensive devices – but no steering wheel!

The Batmobile can only be driven by a person wearing the Batsuit.

Remote controls in the Batsuit allow Terry to pilot the Batmobile from blocks away.

Defenses include smoke projectors and armor plating

Batman only has to move his arms to steer the Batmobile.

BOLA NET

By twirling and hurling this trio of weighted spheres, the Tomorrow Knight can ensnare any enemy in his Bat-Net!

Magnetic Nun Chaku

OTHER WEAPONS

Batman also carries Magnetic Nun Chaku to bash bad guys. Dark Knight Shields repel bullets or blasters. Smoke bombs make villains cough up confessions. Plus, a Dark Knight Staff blocks blows from swords or clubs!

Balancing atop his Rocket-Wing, the Tomorrow Knight surfs into action!

Dark Knight Discus Batarang

Smoke bomb

BAT DATA

• All of Terry's Bat-Gadgets are built and maintained by Bruce Wayne.

• Bat-Gadgets like the Batarang and Bat-Bolas are based on ancient traditional weapons.

THE BATCAVE

When Bruce Wayne retired from fighting crime, the Batcave was mothballed for 20 years. But it didn't take long to put the high-tech headquarters back into action! The Batcave is Batman's base of operations. Here, Bruce Wayne serves as the Tomorrow Knight's guide and mentor, using all the sophisticated equipment at his disposal.

FROM THE CENTRAL computer terminal, Bruce monitors Terry's actions and guides the new Batman through a maze of secret tunnels built by WayneCorp. These passages give Terry fast access to any point in Gotham.

BATCOMPUTER

The Batcave contains the most sophisticated computer system ever built. The Batcomputer stores case files on all Batman's enemies—past, present, and future!

BAT DATA

• The Batcave is located in a system of caverns directly beneath Wayne Manor.

• The Batcave contains trophies taken from villains during Bruce's many years as Batman.

BAT-TIME!

Terry first discovered Batman's underground headquarters after saving Bruce from the Jokerz. When an exhausted Bruce fell asleep in his study, Terry heard a strange noise nearby. It was a bat trapped inside a grandfather clock!

WHEN TERRY FREED the winged creature, he accidentally opened the hidden entrance to the Batcave. That's where the bat had come from! Now Terry understood how Bruce could fight so well. Bruce was really Batman!

THE BATCOMPUTER allows Bruce and Terry to examine critical clues. From fingerprints to tissue samples, the Batcave holds all the equipment the Tomorrow Knight needs to identify and collect incriminating evidence.

THE BAT-FAMILY

Inside the Batcave are all the costumes worn by the Dark Knight and his closest allies. On display are Batman's original Batsuit and the uniforms long ago belonging to Robin (Tim Drake), Batgirl (Barbara Gordon), and Nightwing (Dick Grayson).

FAMILY TIES

In the Batcave's medical bay, Terry learned the truth. Years ago, Bruce's former partner Tim Drake was caught and brainwashed by the Clown Prince of Crime. The Batcave had been wrecked by the man who was once Robin the Boy Wonder!

BRUCE WAYNE

Bruce Wayne may be old, but he hasn't given up on crime fighting just yet! Bruce uses his many years' experience of caped crusading to guide Terry McGinnis as the new Batman. And although Bruce sticks close to the security of the Batcave, he'll don the old Batsuit whenever *two* Batmen are better than one!

ACE IS Bruce Wayne's loyal hound. He guards the estate grounds of Wayne Manor with a fierce bark and a ferocious bite.

LAST HEIR

Bruce is the sole heir to the great Wayne family fortune. He never married and has no known heirs or beneficiaries apart from a few retired sidekicks.

BRUCE WAYNE has been battling injustice for decades. But don't let the cane fool you. Although he's aged and a little arthritic, Bruce can still deliver big blows to bad guys!

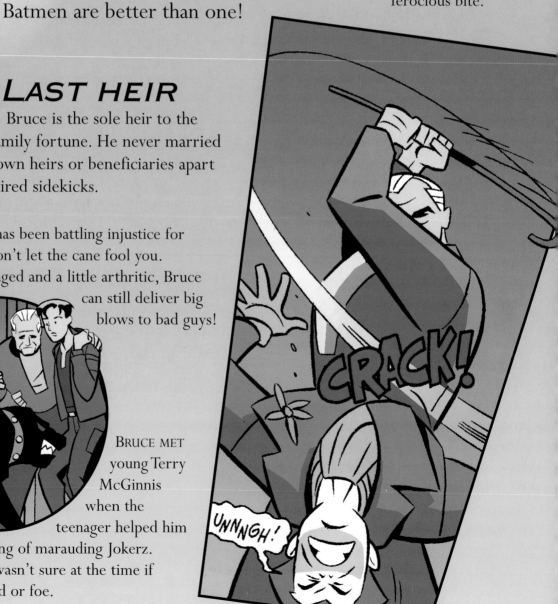

BRUCE MET young Terry McGinnis when the teenager helped him to fight off a gang of marauding Jokerz. However, Ace wasn't sure at the time if Terry was friend or foe.

DURING HIS YEARS as Batman, Bruce mastered many fields of science, particularly chemistry. He can still whip up an anti-toxin to the Joker's laughing gas in no time at all.

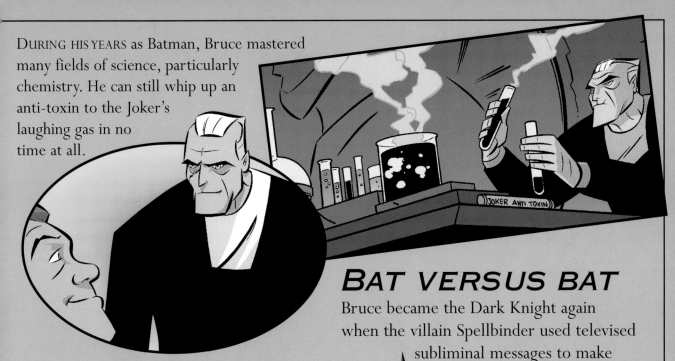

JOKER ANTI TOXIN

BAT VERSUS BAT

Bruce became the Dark Knight again when the villain Spellbinder used televised subliminal messages to make Terry run rampant. The "classic" Caped Crusader was able to show the Tomorrow Knight a few new tricks.

Bruce's last sidekick as Batman was teenager Tim Drake. Tim inherited the role of Robin from Dick Grayson, who became Nightwing as an adult. The former partners eventually reunited when Bruce and Terry saved Tim from the Joker's mind control.

WAYNE-POWERS

Years ago, Bruce Wayne's company was taken over by Derek Powers. Wayne Enterprises was renamed the Wayne-Powers Corporation. Now that Powers is the radioactive menace known as Blight, his scheming son, Paxton Powers, has become chief executive officer of this corporate conglomerate.

BAT DATA
• Bruce Wayne and Barbara Gordon were once romantically linked.

TERRY'S FAMILY

TERRY MCGINNIS

Terry wishes he had spent more quality time with his father instead of constantly bickering. He also wishes he could have prevented his father's murder. As Batman, Terry hopes to honor Warren McGinnis's memory by defending the helpless.

Bruce Wayne had it easier. He never had to juggle home life with the demands of a being a super hero. But Terry McGinnis has a family to worry about. And now that he's the man of the McGinnis house, it's getting harder and harder for Terry to conceal the fact that he's secretly Batman!

SMMOOOCH!

MARY MCGINNIS

Following her husband's death, Terry's widowed mother now works full-time to provide for her two sons. Mary McGinnis is grateful to Terry for helping out with his after-school job "assisting" Bruce Wayne.

TERRY's eight-year-old brother Matt loves video games and idolizes Batman. Often, the McGinnis boys tease and torment each other. Little does Matt know that his older brother and his hero are one and the same!

FAMILY DAY

No matter how busy they are, the McGinnises always find time for "Family Day" fun. Once each month, Mary, Terry, and Matt spend the entire day together, even when Batman has better things to do!

MARY AND MATT know that Terry can be a little weird sometimes. But they just chalk it up to teenage growing pains. For their own safety, Terry makes sure that neither mother nor brother finds out that they're related to the Tomorrow Knight.

WAYNE'S WORLD

Matt McGinnis is Batman?! Well, only in Terry's imagination. Once, Bruce Wayne used hypnosis to implant false memories in Terry's subconscious to fool Spellbinder. The evil trickster had disguised himself as a school psychologist in an attempt to uncover the Dark Knight's identity. Terry's secret alter-ego was preserved because Spellbinder was fooled into believing somebody else was Batman!

FRIENDS AND ALLIES

In the old days, the Dark Knight had a whole host of loyal partners to aid him in his war on crime. The Tomorrow Knight doesn't have a sidekick—yet. But Terry McGinnis does have a few close friends and allies who often lend the new Batman a helping hand.

WHILE TRAILING BLIGHT, Batman met a group of orphans living in the mazelike sewer system beneath Gotham. Terry befriended their leader and protector, Akira. Whenever he can, Batman brings the underground kids food, presents, and all the comforts of home.

DANA TAN

Terry's girlfriend Dana is smart and sassy. She also knows that there is more to Terry's after-school job than meets the eye. Although Terry's constant disappearances annoy her, Dana cares for him very much. Eventually, she might just figure out that her beloved boyfriend is Batman!

FOR DECADES, Jason Blood has advised Bruce Wayne on mystical matters. But Jason doesn't appear to age at all! That's because the magician Merlin once cast a spell on Jason!

ETRIGAN

Like Batman, Jason Blood also has an alter ego. But Etrigan is no costume—he's a real demon! Etrigan once served Merlin in King Arthur's court many centuries ago, but continues to battle monsters and magical menaces unleashed in the 21st century.

Jason Blood's young friend Kyle is no ordinary college student. In addition to his regular course work, Kyle is studying the physics of magic. He invented demonic energy nullifiers and once helped Batman and Etrigan to defeat the diabolical Axilano.

BARBARA GORDON

Barbara Gordon is the top cop in Gotham, just as her father was before her. As the former Batgirl, Barbara knows firsthand how dangerous costumed crime fighting can be. She also knows that Gotham City needs a Batman, whether she likes it or not.

THE GORDON FAMILY

The Gordons have a long history of aiding Batman. As Police Commissioner, James Gordon was once Batman's closest friend. Without Gordon knowing, his daughter Barbara was fighting crime as Batgirl. These days, she's the commish!

JUSTICE LEAGUE UNLIMITED

In the 20th century, Batman belonged to the Justice League of America, a group of the world's greatest super heroes. So it's only fitting that the Tomorrow Knight of the 21st century should join a Justice League Unlimited, featuring some familiar faces and some dynamic new defenders!

Barda

THE WATCHTOWER is the JLU's high-tech headquarters. It's based in Metropolis, the great city guarded by Superman. But with teleporting Boom Tubes courtesy of Barda, the JLU can tackle any threat on Earth in the blink of an eye!

UNLIMITED BACK-UP

Batman isn't a full-time member of Justice League Unlimited. Instead, he prefers to watch over Gotham, and aid the JLU only when it needs him. And the team *really* needs him when it faces arch-foes such as Black Light!

KERSHLAM!

BARDA HAILS from the dark and distant planet Apokolips, home of the evil Darkseid. She is super-strong and wields an energy-blasting Mega-Rod. Barda is married to the master escape artist known as Mister Miracle.

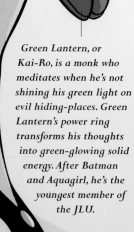

Green Lantern, or Kai-Ro, is a monk who meditates when he's not shining his green light on evil hiding-places. Green Lantern's power ring transforms his thoughts into green-glowing solid energy. After Batman and Aquagirl, he's the youngest member of the JLU.

LIKE HIS PREDECESSOR Hawkman, Warhawk has wings and an anti-gravity belt. Although short-tempered, he is a fierce and formidable fighter. Warhawk and Batman don't always see eye-to-eye. But they always put aside their differences when it's time for teamwork!

Warhawk

LIGHT VS. DARK

The alien adversary Black Light has his own mighty power ring. Was he a former Green Lantern himself? And for what sinister scheme did he force the pacifist Kai-Ro, Earth's latest Green Lantern, into a fight?

Green Lantern normally looks for non-violent ways to subdue super-villains. But even he rises to Black Light's violent taunt and is captured.

THE ATLANTEAN HEROINE Aquagirl can swim like a fish and breathe underwater. Her real name is Mareena.

Aquagirl

GOTHAM OF THE FUTURE

How Gotham has changed in the 21st century! The dirty city is ten times larger and a hundred times more imposing. Buildings loom higher. Cars zoom above the roads. Robots are commonplace. Science fiction has become science fact in the world of the Tomorrow Knight!

MEGALOPOLIS

Gotham was originally built on industry. Charitable companies like Wayne Enterprises were once the backbone of the city. Now, giant corporations are everywhere. Their mile-high buildings eclipse what little sun reaches the streets.

BRUCE WAYNE was forced out of his company in a hostile takeover by the diabolical Derek Powers. However, Bruce made sure he could keep an eye on Powers. The Wayne-Powers Complex has many secret doors known only to Bruce and Batman.

IN GOTHAM, traffic jams are a problem of the past. With the advent of anti-gravity technology, flying vehicles soar high above the ground. Just watch out for those crazy hover-taxi drivers!

Elevated roadways and high-velocity commuter trains link Gotham's mile-high skyscrapers!

IN THE FUTURE, you don't have to exercise to stay fit. For an extreme makeover, some citizens just inject themselves with nanites. These microscopic robots work beneath the skin to make biological adjustments. But sometimes the nanobots develop a life of their own. When that happens, their human hosts act like runaway robots!

SPLICERS

For young Gothamites, the latest craze is to splice animal genes into their own DNA. You could be an alligator-man or a *real* foxy lady. Splicing was made possible by Dr. Abel Cuvier, who once spliced himself with the genes of a tiger, a hawk, and a snake while fighting tooth and claw with Batman!

BAT DATA

• In the future, cash money has been replaced by credit disks.

• Giant construction robots helped to build Gotham's mile-high buildings.

THE JOKERZ

There's no doubt that the Joker was the worst foe Batman ever faced. Happily, the Joker's long gone. Unfortunately, he had the last laugh. Now, giggling gang members wear rubber noses to honor the Clown Prince of Crime. But if it weren't for these hooligans, there wouldn't be a Batman!

J-MAN

Insane in the brain, J-Man is the leader of the Jokerz. He's the only gang member crazy enough to wear the Joker's pinstriped purple tuxedo!

Don't be fooled into thinking that this gang member's flower is just a flower. It shoots a deadly nerve gas!

UNTIL BATMAN came back, the Jokerz ruled the streets of Gotham, terrorizing teenagers like Terry McGinnis and Max Gibson. Too bad the Jokerz didn't know that Terry would soon put a stop their ha-ha-hijinks!

THANKS TO the Tomorrow Knight, new Jokerz recruits are fewer in number. But the remaining comedic crooks are dangerously unpredictable. All it takes is a little bad weather for the Jokerz to start a riot!

SCAB AND DOTTIE

Where J-Man goes, low-class clowns Scab and Dottie are never far behind. Scab dons an oversized punching glove to bop Batman. Dottie makes a real club sandwich with her rubber chicken. A spiked rubber chicken, that is!

BRUCE WAYNE took the Joker very seriously. As Batman, Terry McGinnis also has no sense of humor where the Jokerz are concerned. He'll deck any of these wild cards without cracking a smile.

Watch out, Batman! Dottie's spiky chicken will leave a bad taste in your mouth – a bad taste of blood!

BAT DATA

• Other Jokerz goons include J-Man's second-in-command, Smirk, and the pie-throwing Coe.

RETURN OF THE JOKER

You can't keep a good maniac down! Years ago, the Joker kidnapped and tortured Robin. Batman eventually caught up with the Clown Prince of Crime. But rather than escaping, the Joker electrocuted himself! At last, Batman's most terrible enemy had met his end. Or had he?

BLIGHT

Maniacal mogul Derek Powers had the run of Gotham City until Batman returned to action. The Tomorrow Knight's discovery of the weapons Powers was developing at the Wayne-Powers Corporation led to a fateful fight. In the struggle, Powers was covered in his own caustic chemicals and transformed into the glowing ghoul Blight!

As BLIGHT, Derek Powers is a walking hunk of radioactive waste! One touch from Blight and your skin will burn, blister, and burst!

ARMS DEALER

With his new bio-weapon, Derek Powers was going to make a killing…literally! This terrible tycoon even tested his flesh-eating nerve gas on his own employees! After having Terry McGinnis's father murdered, Powers thought he had taken care of everyone in on his secret.

TERRY McGINNIS used the Batsuit to wreck Powers's nerve gas factory. When Powers tried to stop the Tomorrow Knight with his gun, Batman hurled a nerve gas canister at him. Powers accidentally shot the canister and was doused in the deadly gas!

SPLEW!

BLIGHT CAN HURL balls of radioactive matter from his fingertips. He covers himself in a synthetic skin, but his body's radioactivity eventually breaks down the fake flesh, especially when he gets angry. The madder Blight is, the hotter he burns!

BAT DATA

- Blight's radioactive skin is transparent.
- He is the Tomorrow Knight's most dangerous foe.
- Blight once lived inside an abandoned nuclear submarine.

CASIUM 90

Blight blames Batman for his freakish fate. Now he seeks out radioactive isotopes to fuel his insatiable hunger for energy. The only way the Tomorrow Knight can get close to Blight is by spraying him with Casium 90, an element that renders radioactivity totally harmless.

MELTDOWN

Blight once tried to steal Xanthalium, Yostrium, and Zeliconium – three radioactive elements that would allow him to drain the power from anything! Batman was hot on Blight's trail to prevent a 21st-century energy crisis. And so was the Gamestalker! In the end, Batman covered Blight in molten lead. But Gamestalker zapped Batman and took Blight's inert body home as a hunting trophy!

HOSTILE TAKEOVER

Powers climbed to the top of the corporate ladder by buying out other companies and then firing the chief executives! He forced Bruce Wayne out of Wayne Enterprises and turned the once-benevolent business into a weapons manufacturer!

SHRIEK

Hey, what's that sound? By the time you hear the sonic blasters of Shriek, it could already be too late! Sound engineer Michael Shreeve became a pawn of Derek Powers in order to save his lab from bankruptcy. As the sonic villain Shriek, Shreeve knows how to turn noise into a weapon of mass destruction!

Built-in sonic blasters amplify sound to earth-shattering levels!

HEARING LOSS

Ironically, Michael Shreeve is stone deaf. He is unable to hear any sounds, and so is unaffected by Shriek's sound-suit. Shreeve knows how to read lips, but he turns away from his prison cellmate's constant chatter in order to get a little peace and quiet.

Shriek's sound-suit is made from the advanced alloy acoustium.

WITH THE RIGHT sonic modulation, Shriek's sound generators can bowl over buildings. A certain frequency can even shred his criminal cohort's clothing like paper! Imagine what it would do to the Batsuit!

BATMAN DIDN'T know it, but Shriek saved a Batarang from his last scuffle with the Tomorrow Knight. Patiently, the villain searched for the correct vibrational frequency to shatter Batman's weapons with white noise!

SOUND OFF!

The next time they battled, Shriek tried to deafen Batman with his sound generators. Unfortunately for Terry, bats have big ears!

THE BATSUIT COULD only muffle so much! Numbed by the noise, Terry was helpless as Shriek sounded off and overloaded the circuits inside the Tomorrow Knight's high-tech costume.

Shriek's sound masker creates total silence, allowing him to creep up on Batman unheard!

SHRIEK MAY HAVE figured out how to destroy the Tomorrow Knight's gadgets, but Terry also came armed with the original Batman's tools-of-the-trade. Shriek didn't have time to re-modulate his sound generators to rock a "classic" Batarang!

BAT DATA

• The Tomorrow Knight relied on Ace's acute canine hearing to track down Shriek.

• Shriek once drove Gotham's animals into a frenzy by sending screeching soundwaves across the city!

LISTEN TO THE MUSIC

Terry knew that the only way to silence Shriek was to make him listen to his own staggering sound waves! Overloaded by its own power, Shriek's sound-suit self-destructed!

INQUE

Inque is the most slippery super-villain the Tomorrow Knight has faced so far. Once a beautiful young woman, Inque became a shape-shifting saboteur after being subjected to mutagenic experiments. Now she's a living liquid who pours herself into her work!

LIQUIDITY

Mutagenic experiments transformed Inque into a polymorph. She can mold her body into any shape imaginable. In her liquid form, it's easy for Inque to slip through tight ventilation ducts or slide right under locked doors.

WARNING
PASS KEY
ONLY

BATMAN FIRST fought Inque after Derek Powers hired the crafty corporate spy. She made her mark by blotting out a business rival!

WHEN YOU'RE polymorphic like Inque, it's easy to shape-shift yourself into a living weapon. Watch out, Batman… it's hammer time!

INQUE'S ONLY problem with being a liquid lady is that she sometimes leaves drops of herself behind following a fight. Terry scooped up a sample of Inque and took it back to the Batcave for Bruce Wayne to analyze.

- Inque's real name is unknown, perhaps even to her!

- To defeat Inque, Batman and Bruce Wayne fought her with a fire-hose and then stopped her cold with Mr. Freeze's Freeze Gun.

AN EVIL scientist developed special implants that helped Inque to regain some solidity. But Inque had to commit crimes to pay him back, and suffered his wrath when she didn't deliver what he wanted!

CORPORATE SPY

Inque sells her skills to the highest bidder, but only to raise funds to find a cure for her condition. She hacks into computers for any information that might make her whole again.

USUALLY, INQUE can maintain a measure of solidity. By the time the evil scientist figured out how to make her half-liquid body melt into a puddle, Batman was on *her* side!

DIPPED IN INQUE

One of Inque's strangest powers is the ability to envelop someone with a thin coating of her viscous body and make that person do her  bidding! Is that a spot on your suit…or are you covered in Inque?!

GAMESTALKER

Gamestalker hunts the world's most dangerous prey, be it man or beast. Unfortunately, that includes the Tomorrow Knight! To prove his superior tracking skills, Gamestalker often tricks Batman into becoming his target.

GAMESTALKER prefers to hunt barehanded. Other than his own bionic body, Gamestalker's favorite weapon is his electrified pike. It stuns his prey senseless before Gamestalker makes the kill.

BIG GAME

When Terry McGinnis and his friends found themselves on Gamestalker's island of dino-animals, Terry had to make a difficult decision: Hunt or be hunted!

As Batman, Terry bravely tried to subdue the savage beasts before Gamestalker slaughtered everyone.

Gamestalker's bionic body allows him to leap enormous distances in pursuit of his prey.

GAMESTALKER knows Terry's secret identity. Other foes would gleefully use this knowledge to terrorize the Tomorrow Knight. But despite his hobby of hunting Batman whenever possible, Gamestalker isn't considered a true enemy.

Powerful bionic hands can kill prey with one clench!

GAMESTALKER'S CAREER as a professional big game hunter ended when a ferocious black panther mauled him. His wounded body was repaired with bionic parts. Now he's as strong as ten men and possesses heightened senses. Gamestalker can see, hear, or smell prey from miles away!

ONE OF GAMESTALKER'S eyes contains electronic crosshairs that draw a bionic bead on his targets. Gamestalker won't use firearms, but he's a dead shot with a tranquilizing dart gun!

TROPHY ROOM

Gamestalker's trophy room looks more like a cave! Inside, there are all sorts of exotic creatures stuffed and mounted so that Gamestalker can relive the thrill of his hunts. His most recent catches include the lead-encased Blight and a hybrid Hippo-Rex!

BAT DATA

• Gamestalker was once employed by the U.S. government to hunt down the criminal known as False Face.

ROYAL FLUSH GANG

A team of professional thieves, the Royal Flush Gang isn't playing with a full deck! This family of fiends always tries to deal Batman a losing hand. However, the Tomorrow Knight can think of *ten* reasons why *one* of these cardsharps isn't all bad!

THE ROYAL FLUSH GANG is a family affair, with father King, mother Queen, son Jack, daughter Ten, and an android Ace up their sleeves. The Gang raises the stakes of villainy by riding into action atop flying playing cards!

52 PICK-UP

King swings a sword. Queen has a scepter. Jack likes daggers. Otherwise, the Gang's weapons are all concealed as cards. Better fold, Batman! Jack's hand could include razor-sharp blades, smoke bombs, or even a full house of high-explosives!

THE ROYAL FLUSH GANG'S Ten is a pretty teenaged girl named Melanie Walker. After falling in love with Terry, she tried to give up crime. Once, an impostor Royal Flush Gang tried to bluff Batman into thinking Melanie was back to being bad!

TEN HAS had no luck convincing her family to throw in their cards and rehabilitate. If she turns her life around, Terry might just be there for her when she gets out of jail.

Ma Mayhem

The Mayhems are another family of related rogues. Ma Mayhem is the leader, a malicious matriarch who doesn't spare the rod when she spoils her slow-witted sons. The Mayhem bunch specializes in jailbreaks and jewel heists!

A WICKED WIDOW, Ma Mayhem is as strong as she is mean. Suffering anxiety from being separated from her sons, Ma planned her own bold breakout from prison!

CARL AND SLIM

The Mayhem boys are totally loyal to their Ma. Big and tall Carl is the muscle of the gang. Short and mousy Slim Mayhem always drives the getaway hovercar.

CARL AND SLIM know better than to sass their Ma. First it's a slap. After that, they'll get a real lickin'!

The Mayhems added abduction to their rap sheet when they kidnapped Princess Vinishri of Uganistan. Thankfully, Batman was close behind to liberate her from these folksy felons!

SPELLBINDER

Dizzying and diabolical, the Spellbinder hypnotizes his victims into having haunting hallucinations! Even Batman isn't immune to the Spellbinder's ocular orb. This floating eyeball can transfix the Tomorrow Knight and make him do the bad guy's bidding!

MESMERIZED!

Spellbinder is really former Hamilton Hill High School psychologist Dr. Ira Billings. Billings got tired of being underpaid and unappreciated, so he took to spellbinding his students in order to make himself rich. Under Spellbinder's thrall, even peaceable people are forced to bash the Tomorrow Knight!

BATMAN STOPPED the Spellbinder's scheme of hypnotizing rich high school kids into revealing where their family jewels and wealth were hidden. Later, Spellbinder placed subliminal messages in television broadcasts to mesmerize the Tomorrow Knight!

SOMEHOW, SPELLBINDER figured out that the Tomorrow Knight was a teenager. In disguise, Dr. Ira Billings used his mind-reading machine to give psychic profiles to students he believed might secretly be Batman!

Spellbinder's costume is covered in hypnotic patterns designed to mesmerize anyone who sees him!

TERMINAL

As the teen terror Terminal, Carter Wilson once led a rebel rabble of Jokerz. Psychotherapy helped Carter to bury this sinister side deep inside his brain. However, Terminal was just waiting for the right time to tear Carter apart!

CARTER WILSON went to Hamilton Hill High School with Terry McGinnis and Max Gibson. As Terminal, Carter once threatened Max's life. Max forgave Carter after he had served his sentence and defeated his dark side.

WHEN CARTER successfully separated his good side from his bad side, Terminal took over! Pretty soon, Terminal's gang of Jokerz were back in action blasting Batman silly with their gag guns!

TWO-FACED

Batman beat Terminal by appealing to the goodness left in Carter. In the end, Carter went back to Juvenile Hall. Terminal and Carter are now divided right down the middle. Each constantly clash for control of Carter's body and soul!

THE ASSASSINS

It's bad enough that the Tomorrow Knight has enough enemies to fill an entire prison. But then there's also the Society of Assassins, a plethora of professional killers! And there's rivalry among the Society's members to be the one skilled enough to slay Batman!

CURARÉ

Stealthy as a shadow and nimble as a ninja, Curaré is armed with a scimitar that can slice through anything. Batman first fought this lady killer when she tried to terminate D.A. Sam Young, Commissioner Barbara Gordon's husband!

Curaré will sometimes throw her blade with deadly accuracy if she can't get close enough to stab!

IT'S NOT EASY catching a sword between your hands before it cuts you in half! But Batman knows just how to stop Curaré's scimitar, even when another assassin is wielding the deadly blade.

SECRET SOCIETY

To join the Society of Assassins, new bloods must prove their worthiness by spilling blood: Batman's! Curaré ranks highest among this killer elite and is the Society's leader. The penalty for failing her is death!

CURARÉ'S SCIMITAR can slice concrete or steel like a hot knife through butter! Only Society members may wield it. And they would rather die themselves than let an outsider like Batman defile their sacred sword!

BAT DATA

• Curaré is incredibly fast and agile. She knows many martial-arts skills.

KOBRA

The cult of Kobra has existed for centuries. The Dark Knight fought it during his crime-fighting career. And now the Tomorrow Knight continues the struggle to stop these terrorists once and for all!

KOBRAS WORSHIP chaos and aim to bring anarchy and Armageddon to the 21st century. The Kobra cult has thousands of scaly soldiers slithering about to make this bad dream come true.

SERPENT EGGS

Some soldiers join Kobra willingly. Others are shanghaied into this serpent society! Batman stopped Kobra from kidnapping Gotham's homeless people and brainwashing them into converting to the cult.

KOBRAS WEAR gloves with a poisonous touch! This mind-bending snake serum could make the Tomorrow Knight into a Kobra soldier. Thank goodness the Batsuit is impermeable to venom!

SOME KOBRA cultists carry electrified snake-staffs. To his dismay, Batman discovered that there's no cure for this blazing bite!

BAT DATA

• A Kobra agent once abducted Terry McGinnis's friend Max Gibson into a forced marriage!

41

DEMONS

Some say that Gotham City is a magnet for evil. Occasionally, it even becomes a gateway to the underworld! Terry McGinnis has seen some strange things as Batman, including a whole host of nightmarish demons!

THE FIRST DEMON Batman ever encountered was Axilano. This dark devil was once imprisoned by Merlin the Magician. But what was he doing in 21st-century Gotham City?

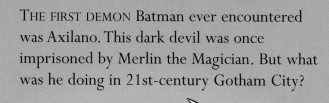

TEENAGER PRESTON LEEDS was responsible for unleashing Axilano on an unsuspecting Gotham. Preston was researching Merlin's book of spells on his computer and accidentally cast one himself. Axilano and Preston were hopelessly bound together!

DIGIMAGIC

To subdue Axilano, Batman called upon Bruce Wayne's old friend Jason Blood and a young college student named Kyle. By mixing old magic with new, Jason Blood's demonic alter ego Etrigan joined Batman to fight Axilano while Kyle trapped the devil inside a digital dungeon.

BATMAN LEARNED the hard way that Axilano wasn't easy to punch! The demon could make himself as immaterial as a phantom when struck, or as hard as rock when he wanted to strike back!

BAT DATA

- All the magical power of the Dark Universe is at Axilano's command.

VENDETTA

There were many who hated Derek Powers's evil son Paxton, but Vendetta wanted revenge against him more than most. No one was going to stop her getting justice for his betrayal of her. And that included Batman!

At first, neither the Tomorrow Knight nor Powers realized that the truth behind Vendetta's identity was closer than they thought!

MISS WINSTON

Paxton Powers ordered the death of Miss Winston, his father's secretary, because she knew too much about his crimes. But she didn't die! Unknown to everybody, she was in fact Vendetta, imbued with superpowers!

BIGGER AND STRONGER than most men, Vendetta was a fierce fighter, too! Bullets simply bounced right off her body and only made her madder!

THOUGH NO ONE heard her, Vendetta once confessed her love for Derek Powers. She even sacrificed her own well-being to protect the Wayne-Powers Corporation. While fighting Batman, her glowing tears fell like acid onto the toxic power-sticks and ignited an inferno!

VENDETTA WAS determined to stop Powers from shipping dangerous power-stick batteries. Made from two inert gases, the power-sticks gave off poisonous fumes when the gases were mixed. Vendetta hijacked a hover-truck and terrorized its drivers to prevent such an outcome!

ROGUES GALLERY

Blight, the Jokerz, and Shriek aren't the only offenders Batman has to worry about in his future world. The Rogues Gallery keeps growing with all-new foes, including the following felonious fiends.

MR. FREEZE

Derek Powers thawed out villain Victor Fries from suspended animation. Unfortunately, Fries still needed low temperatures to survive. That's why Mr. Freeze returned with an icy vengeance!

STINGER THINKS he's the bee's knees with his high-tech flight suit and barbed-dart launchers. But after aiming too many bad puns at Batman, Stinger himself was stung and swatted.

Freeze stops his enemies dead in their tracks with an icy shot from his cryo-blaster.

RATBOY PATRICK Fitz can control rats and mice. He once kidnapped Terry's girlfriend Dana Tan because he had a crush on her. After his face was burned in a fight with Batman, Fitz tried to alter his rodentlike appearance. Dana still wouldn't go out with him, though!

BAT DATA

• Blight cracked open Victor Fries's cryo-suit, which then exploded and apparently destroyed the long-suffering Mr. Freeze.

THE MUMMY

The ancient mummified madman Tetlecteloti came back to life for the sake of his princess bride, Dayh-Neh. However, this mummy thought Terry's girlfriend Dana was the reincarnation of his true love!

ERICA ELECTRA

Erica Grace isn't evil at all, but she did fall foul of Batman once. Armed with anti-gravity boot-disks and super-charged shocker-gloves, she became Erica Electra in order to force Dr. Roberto Varkony into admitting that he had stolen scientific designs from her father.

THE GOLEM

Originally, the Golem was a GLM construction robot, mind-controlled by twisted teenager Willie Watt. The second Golem was a walking pile of scrap metal assembled by Morgan Bickford after authorities unjustly separated Morgan from his father.

BAT DATA

• Bullying by his father and fellow students drove Willie Watt to seek revenge with the giant robot, Golem.

GAZETTEER

Aquagirl (voiced by Jodi Benson)
First appeared in THE CALL, Part One
(Episode #46).

Barda (voiced by Farrah Forke)
First appeared in THE CALL, Part One
(Episode #46).

Bruce Wayne Batman (voiced by Kevin
Conroy)
First appeared in REBIRTH, Part One
(Episode #1).

Commissioner Barbara Gordon (voiced by
Stockard Channing and Angie Harmon)
First appeared in REBIRTH, Part One
(Episode #1).

Curaré (voiced by Melissa Disney)
First appeared in A TOUCH OF CURARÉ
(Episode #12).

D.A. Sam Young (voiced by Paul Winfield)
First appeared in A TOUCH OF CURARÉ
(Episode #12).

Dana Tan (voiced by Lauren Tom)
First appeared in REBIRTH, Part One
(Episode #1).

Derek Powers/Blight (voiced by Sherman
Howard)
First appeared in REBIRTH, Part One
(Episode #1).

Dr. Abel Cuvier (voiced by Ian Buchanan)
First appeared in SPLICERS
(Episode #14).

Dr. Stephanie Lake (voiced by Linda
Hamilton)
First appeared in MELTDOWN
(Episode #5).

Gamestalker (voiced by Carl Lumbly)
First appeared in BLOOD SPORT
(Episode #19).

Green Lantern (voiced by Lauren Tom)
First appeared in THE CALL, Part One
(Episode #46).

Inque (voiced by Shannon Kenny)
First appeared in BLACK OUT
(Episode #3).

Jack (voiced by Scott Cleverdon)
First appeared in DEAD MAN'S HAND
(Episode #8).

King (voiced by George Lazenby)
First appeared in DEAD MAN'S HAND
(Episode #8).

Ma Mayhem (voiced by Kathleen Freeman)
First appeared in THE EGGBABY
(Episode #32).

Mary McGinnis (voiced by Terri Garr)
First appeared in REBIRTH, PART ONE
(Episode #1).

Matt McGinnis (voiced by Ryan
O'Donohue)
First appeared in REBIRTH, Part One
(Episode #1).

Max Gibson (voiced by Cree Summer)
First appeared in HIDDEN AGENDA
(Episode #18).

Micron (voiced by Wayne Brady)
First appeared in THE CALL, Part One
(Episode #46).

Mr. Fixx (voiced by George Takei)
First appeared in REBIRTH, Part One
(Episode #1).

Patrick Fitz/Ratboy (voiced by Taran Noah
Smith)

First appeared in RATS (Episode #22).

Paxton Powers (voiced by Cary Elwes and
Parker Stevenson)
First appeared in ASCENSION
(Episode #13).

Queen (voiced by Amanda Donohoe)
First appeared in DEAD MAN'S HAND
(Episode #8).

Shriek/Walter Shreeve (voiced by Chris
Mulkey)
First appeared in SHRIEK (Episode #7).

Spellbinder (voiced by Jon Cypher)
First appeared in SPELLBOUND
(Episode #8).

Superman (voiced by Christopher
McDonald)
First appeared in THE CALL, Part One
(Episode #46).

Ten/Melanie Walker (voiced by Olivia
D'Abo)
First appeared in DEAD MAN'S HAND
(Episode #8).

Terminal/Carter Wilson (voiced by
Michael Rosenbaum)
First appeared in HIDDEN AGENDA
(Episode #18).

Terry McGinnis/Batman (voiced by Will
Friedle)
First appeared in REBIRTH, PART ONE
(Episode #1).

Victor Fries/Mister Freeze (voiced by
Michael Ansara)
First appeared in MELTDOWN
(Episode #5).

Warhawk (voiced by Peter Onorati)
First appeared in THE CALL, Part One
(Episode #46).

Warren McGinnis (voiced by Michael
Gross)
First appeared in REBIRTH, Part One
(Episode #1).

Willie Watt/Golem (voiced by Scott
McAfee)
First appeared in GOLEM (Episode #4).

INDEX

ACKNOWLEDGMENTS

Dorling Kindersley would like to thank the following DC artists for their contributions to this book:

Terry Beatty, Rick Burchett, Dan Davis, Jordi Ensign, Min S. Ku, Rob Leigh, Ande Parks, Sean Parsons, Craig Rousseau, and Joe Staton.

The author would like to gratefully thank:
Steve Korté, Alastair Dougall, Robert Perry, Jon Richards,
Chris Cerasi, and Jennifer Myskowski.

Dorling Kindersley would like to thank:
Steve Korté and Chris Cerasi at DC Comics.